I'M GOOD AT
SPORT
WHAT JOB CAN I GET?

Richard Spilsbury

WAYLAND

First published in 2013 by Wayland
Copyright © Wayland 2013

Wayland
338 Euston Road
London NW1 3BH

Wayland Australia
Level 17/207
Kent Street
Sydney, NSW 2000

Produced for Wayland by
White-Thomson Publishing Ltd
www.wtpub.co.uk
+44 (0)843 2087 460

Editor: Kelly Davis
Designer: Tim Mayer
Picture research: Richard Spilsbury
Proofreader and indexer: Lucy Ross

Dewey categorisation: 796'.023-dc23

ISBN-13: 9780750280082

Printed in China

10 9 8 7 6 5 4 3 2 1

Wayland is a division of Hachette
Children's Books, an Hachette UK company.
www.hachette.co.uk

Picture credits
1, Shutterstock/Maxim Petrichuk; 3,
Dreamstime/Paparazzofamily; 4, Dreamstime/
Pniesen; 5, Dreamstime/Teconley; 6,
Dreamstime/Aykuterd; 7, Dreamstime/Rixie;
8, Dreamstime/Irynarasko; 9, Dreamstime/
CandyBox; 10, Dreamstime/Paparazzofamily;
11, Shutterstock/katatonia82; 12,
Dreamstime/Mondan80; 13, Shutterstock/
Rena Schild; 14, Dreamstime/Rosedarc; 15,
Dreamstime/Andresr; 16, Dreamstime/
Grosremy; 17, Dreamstime/ Denyskuvaiev; 18,
Dreamstime/StuartPearcey; 19, Dreamstime/
Taskeng; 20, Dreamstime/Dylanjones; 21,
Dreamstime/Neeila; 22 Shutterstock/PathomP;
23, Shutterstock/Maxim Petrichuk; 24,
Dreamstime/Arenacreative; 25, Shutterstock/
Pressmaster; 26, Dreamstime/Scarlett070;
27, Dreamstime/Masuti; 28, Dreamstime/
Orangeline; 29, Dreamstime/Chris Van Lennep
Photo; cover (top left), Shutterstock/Fotokostic;
cover (top right), Shutterstock/arek_malang;
cover (bottom), Shutterstock/Gabi Moisa.

CONTENTS

The world of sport

Scoring the winning goal, beating the world record, swimming a length or taking part in a fun run. These are just a few of the reasons people get involved in, and are motivated by, sport. Some can also use their sporting skills and interest in their careers.

The importance of sport

Taking part in sport at any age offers many benefits. Sport helps us stay fit, which keeps us healthy. It also relaxes and calms us. Performing and competing can make us better at coping with pressure. A sports match can provide a controlled outlet for any aggression we may be feeling. In addition, meeting and being active alongside others can make us more sociable.

Learning and perfecting a sport requires determination, and allows us to develop skills and techniques, learn to follow rules and maintain our fitness.

Becoming an elite athlete can bring not only personal glory, but also fame, fortune and opportunities to travel the world.

Sport in the workplace

Sports skills can be useful in any career, helping us to be prepared, achieve, compete and do our best. Today, many people are getting involved in sport and keeping fit, and enjoy attending and watching sports events. There's a wide range of opportunities in the world of sports and leisure to meet this demand. Read on to learn about some of the sports-related jobs out there.

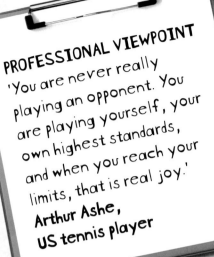

Special skills

If you are keen on sport, you are likely to be self-motivated, self-disciplined and willing to work hard in order to achieve your best. You probably love challenges and may have a competitive nature and be mentally tough. Sportspeople often handle pressure well. They generally understand the value of teamwork and the importance of preparation and good time management.

↓ Sport is for everyone, no matter what age or ability. The goals are always to take part, compete, do your best and have fun!

Sports physiotherapist

Would you like to help other people enjoy or succeed at sport by overcoming their injuries, health and physical difficulties? If so, becoming a sports physiotherapist could be an enjoyable future for you.

Different types of sports physiotherapist

Some sports physiotherapists work with professional sportspeople or teams. They may do anything from taping a gymnast's wrists, to prevent strain, to providing rehabilitation for a footballer with a broken leg. They may work as part of a team, with sports coaches and other support staff. Many sports physiotherapists work in private or NHS clinics, carrying out specialised treatments, such as ultrasound or massage, for a wide range of clients. Some have private practices but others work as part of a team in health and fitness clubs or leisure centres.

Job description

Sports physiotherapists:
- examine, diagnose and work out the causes of injuries
- plan treatment programmes with patients and sports teams
- use a wide range of treatments, from manipulation of joints to acupuncture
- assess progress and agree a realistic timescale for the sportsperson to return to full activity
- keep records of treatment and progress.

It takes skill to help people recover and feel confident in their physical abilities after injury.

Physiotherapists are on hand at sports matches to deal with injuries as soon as they arise.

What skills do I need?

To become a sports physiotherapist, people generally study A-level biology or BTEC health studies at college before taking a physiotherapy degree. You need an interest in sports techniques, along with good communication skills. It is vital to be patient, tactful and understanding with your patients, who will often be in pain and deeply frustrated as a result of their injuries.

PROFESSIONAL VIEWPOINT

'I like the daily variety of lots of different situations and the contact with lots of different people. Of course I like helping people overcome their problems. Being a sports physio is often about helping people to achieve their goals, their dreams even.'

Kim Saha, physiotherapist in a private clinic

Fitness instructor

Think of the variety of people using a sports centre or gym each day in order to get fitter. Fitness instructors lead and organise group and individual exercise programmes to help people achieve this. They make exercise safe, fun and productive.

Job description

Fitness instructors:

- assess new clients and plan personal programmes of exercise based on agreed health and fitness goals
- demonstrate and supervise safe and effective use of exercise apparatus
- lead group exercise classes, such as circuit training, aerobics or spinning
- check and record clients' progress, for example by measuring heart rate and body fat
- give advice on healthy eating and lifestyle.

↑ Personal trainers can help maximise a client's exercise regime in a variety of settings, indoor and out.

Different types of fitness instructor

Some fitness instructors oversee a range of activities, from weight training to treadmills. Others offer particular classes, such as keep fit, aquacise (exercise in water) or yoga in a variety of sports centres and other places. Many fitness instructors work with several clients at once, but some are personal trainers working with one individual. Other fitness instructors work with specific groups of people, such as older adults, children, people with disabilities or those who have been referred by doctors.

'I never give up on anyone. Some trainers think that if a client can't be bothered then they're not worth it, but I think that's the real job of being a personal trainer. Part trainer, part counsellor, part big brother!'

James Hardy,
personal trainer

What skills do I need?

To become a fitness instructor, you need to know how the body works, from muscles to heart rate. Many instructors take certificates or diplomas in fitness, exercise or personal training instruction (recognised by the Register of Exercise Professionals) to prove their expertise. You may be very keen on fitness yourself, with personal experience of health and fitness training. You will also need to be confident, outgoing and supportive in order to motivate your clients to get fitter.

Motivating a class of individuals to develop stamina, confidence and self-esteem is one of the rewards of being a fitness instructor.

Sports journalist

Are you passionate about sports statistics, sports current affairs and watching sport events? And do you like to tell other people all about them? Then you are an ideal candidate for a job as a sports journalist.

↑ Sport is ever changing and unpredictable and can make history. Journalists are on hand to tell the world as it happens.

Job description

Sports journalists:
- research useful sporting statistics and facts
- interview sportspeople and team managers
- watch matches and write reports or reviews for newspapers, magazines or online articles
- create scripts and research unscripted information to use during gaps in the action for live broadcasts
- commentate on sporting action
- constantly improve their knowledge of sports teams, players and statistics.

Different types of sports journalist

Some sports journalists write a newspaper, magazine or online column. They mainly report the results and action from recent matches, bouts or tournaments for a particular sport. They may also research pieces about general developments within the sport, such as match fixing or new sporting equipment. Other sports journalists are commentators who broadcast play-by-play action and opinions from live matches on TV, radio or the Internet. They may interview sports personalities and experts.

→

At a major sports event, there may be many sports journalists reporting for media around the world.

What skills do I need?

Many sports journalists have a degree in journalism, sports journalism, communications or public relations (PR) but experience is vital to get a job in this field. Some sports journalists start writing or presenting sports fixtures for a college or local radio station or newspaper. Like other reporters, sports journalists should be able to communicate well, research relevant information, be well organised, and able to work under pressure and meet deadlines. It helps to be interested in many different sports at first, because you may be asked to report on athletics one day, tennis the next and football the day after that!

Sports official

Sports officials take control of sporting events or competitions. Their job is to help decide winners and losers. They make sure that players follow the rules of the game and play safely to avoid injuring other players or spectators.

Job description

Sports officials:
- start races, matches and competitions
- judge performances and award points or goals
- impose penalties on participants who break rules
- keep track of scores and event duration
- work with other match officials
- report to regulating bodies on events in a match, including disciplinary measures.

A football referee warns a player for fouling another. Referees often co-operate with linespeople to oversee matches across large pitches.

Different types of sports official

Sports officials often specialise in one sport, such as hockey, tennis or boxing. Some of them become referees or umpires, who make final sporting decisions. Others are line judges who, for example, confirm whether a ball lands in or out of play on a tennis court. Sports officials may specialise at different levels within the sport – for instance, they might referee minor league rather than international matches.

What skills do I need?

Most sports officials have had experience of playing their chosen sport and care passionately about it. Many volunteer to officiate at amateur sports events to gain experience and get certificates from professional sporting bodies (such as FIFA), proving their abilities. Good officials need to be decisive and confident. They should be alert and fit, to keep up with the sporting action, and be prepared to work indoors and out, whatever the weather, often at night and weekends.

↑ Sports officials know the rules inside out so they can deal calmly with competitive or argumentative sportspeople challenging their decisions.

Sports centre manager

Many activities go on in the average sports centre or gym, and there are lots of staff members working there and customers making use of the equipment. If you take this up as a career, you will be responsible for the day-to-day running of a centre with sport and leisure facilities.

↓ A public swimming pool manager attracts customers by providing instructors and lifeguards. They also need to ensure that water is treated to keep it clean.

PROFESSIONAL VIEWPOINT

'I am passionate about providing the best possible service at all times. Although it is very difficult to please every customer – and the manager is the person customers complain to – I always try to retain a sense of humour to help motivate staff and provide a welcoming atmosphere for customers.'

Tarzem, gym manager

What skills do I need?

Sports centre managers should be interested in physical fitness and have good information technology (IT), marketing and communication skills. They must be able to put together and motivate excellent teams of staff. Some managers have a degree in a subject such as sports and leisure management, leisure studies or sports science. Others build up experience and expertise as a member of staff while working towards professional qualifications in a sports centre.

↓ Sports centre managers plan and co-ordinate the facilities and fitness classes that the public want.

Different types of sports centre manager

Managers work in many different settings. These range from indoor swimming pools, climbing walls and velodromes to outdoor dry ski-runs, golf courses and sports arenas. The manager will usually work in an office, deciding on the range of courses to offer, employing instructors and other staff, ensuring that equipment and facilities are safe, and promoting the centre in order to encourage customers to use it.

Job description

Sports centre managers:

- arrange timetables for sporting activities
- recruit, train and manage staff
- control budgets
- ensure that health and safety regulations are met at all times
- attract customers with marketing efforts such as special promotions
- organise repairs, refurbishment and upgrading of facilities
- react to changes in customer demand, such as putting on Zumba classes.

Sports psychologist

Many sportspeople experience dips in form, injuries, pressure to succeed, bad publicity and other issues during their careers that make them question their abilities. Sports psychologists help them develop the mental tools they need to cope with these problems and achieve their sporting goals.

→ A sports psychologist can help an athlete develop the self-belief to carry on when they feel like giving up.

→ When an athlete is seriously injured, a sports psychologist helps them to cope mentally with the slow recovery, and period of inactivity, before they can perform again.

PROFESSIONAL VIEWPOINT

'I am only teaching the mental skills part of the time. Most of the time I am just dealing with the human being in front of me, trying to help them deal with things in their life that may be holding them back from achieving higher performance.'

Dr Sean Richardson, sports psychologist

Different types of sports psychologist

Some sports psychologists work with individual athletes in one or more different sports disciplines, often as freelancers. Others may have full-time jobs enhancing performance in entire sports teams, from players to coaches, alongside nutritionists, physiotherapists and other specialists. Some also teach and research sports psychology at university, or advise sporting organisations on how to use psychological techniques to achieve better sports results.

What skills do I need?

To become a sports psychologist you will need to be very good at science, as well as having some practical experience in sports performance, such as coaching. Most sports psychologists have undergraduate and postgraduate degrees in psychology or related subjects, but not in sports or exercise. They will also have professional experience gained through working with other sports psychologists. You should be a sympathetic listener, and enjoy communicating with others.

Lifeguard

People sometimes get into trouble in the water (for example, when they are swimming or surfing) and may risk drowning. Lifeguards make sure that swimmers are safe by preventing accidents and responding to emergencies.

Job description

Lifeguards:
- patrol and watch a pool or beach, watching out for swimmers in difficulties
- identify hazards and advise people on where and when they can swim safely
- enforce pool and beach rules
- use surfboards, jet skis or boats to reach people who have got into difficulty
- use life-saving techniques in emergencies
- give first aid if necessary.

Different types of lifeguard

Most lifeguards work in sport and leisure centres, private fitness clubs or hotels. They enforce pool safety rules, help distressed swimmers, give first aid and check the temperature and hygiene of the water. Other lifeguards work on beaches, making sure that people remain in areas that are safe from hazards such as strong tides and rocks, and responding fast to dangerous situations at sea.

→ Beach lifeguards position flags to show the public where it is safe to swim. They are trained to quickly reach and rescue swimmers who get into trouble.

Lifeguards practise their rescue skills in pools so they know what to do in a real emergency.

What skills do I need?

You must be a strong swimmer, and physically fit in order to help people to safety, some of whom will be panicking. You should be able to communicate calmly, clearly and with authority. To become a lifeguard, you will need certificates from the Royal Life Saving Society, Royal National Lifeboat Institution or Swimming Teachers' Association, including National Rescue Standard qualifications. In this job there can be long periods with not much happening, but you still have to remain alert for the whole of your shift

PROFESSIONAL VIEWPOINT
'I get to meet and work with many interesting people. I like helping customers stay safe and enjoy themselves at the same time. Working as a lifeguard enables me to keep fit and to progress to other roles within the leisure industry.'
Ian Prosser, lifeguard

19

Outdoor activities instructor

Do your sporting and fitness interests involve pony trekking, climbing or canoeing, rather than badminton or rowing machines? Do you like to get others involved in enjoying the great outdoors too? Then you might like to become an outdoor activities instructor.

Job description

Outdoor activities instructors:

- plan activities to suit the needs, abilities and experience of each group
- explain and demonstrate activities
- instruct in one or more specialist areas, such as sailing or climbing
- make sure that all equipment and facilities are safe
- explain safety and emergency procedures
- check weather conditions before starting sessions, assess hazards and manage risks.

↑ Instructors enable people to have thrilling outdoor experiences, such as white water rafting, while making sure they are safe by preparing well and choosing the right routes and equipment.

Some instructors work in open countryside with natural features such as mountains, caves and rivers, or in outdoor education centres with man-made facilities like climbing walls. They may run short one-day or residential courses in one location or lead national or international expeditions. Instructors teach techniques such as abseiling, and safety aspects (for example, the importance of helmets). They encourage customers to try new activities and to work together to complete challenges, for instance in team-building sessions for companies.

→ Instructors can get an overwhelming sense of achievement when they help someone challenge themselves and achieve something new.

What skills do I need?

Most instructors have coaching qualifications approved by the relevant national governing body for their specialist sport or activity. You will need first aid and life-saving certificates for water-based activities. Some outdoor education instructors have an outdoor education or sports degree, but some do not. Instructors should be physically fit and good at motivating, encouraging and passing on skills to others. They often work long hours, including weekends and public holidays, and some jobs (like that of skiing instructor) may be seasonal.

Sports engineer

What have the dimples on a golf ball and the suspension on a mountain bike got in common? They are both technological solutions developed by sports engineers in order to improve sports performance.

Sports engineers design and test sports equipment used by athletes in order to help them go faster, improve their endurance, or gain more power or accuracy. These engineers can work on anything – from carbon-fibre blades amputees use to run, to a new fabric for goalkeepers' gloves that stiffens for protection when the ball hits it.

Testing materials in labs for use in equipment in the real world is part of a sports engineer's job.

Engineers may test material properties and use computer modelling to design these products. They also study athletes' movement and sporting behaviour to see how this can be enhanced using technology.

Job description

Sports engineers:
• assess, design and build new equipment, based on athletes' requirements
• work in labs, testing equipment and devising new materials
• use computer modelling to simulate the forces acting on athletes and their equipment
• test prototypes in real-life sports situations – for example, by watching video recordings of how rackets twist when hitting a ball
• collaborate with sports manufacturers to create new products.

> **PROFESSIONAL VIEWPOINT**
> 'Students who work for me and have a passion for sports – particularly the sport they are working on – tend to be far more productive.'
> **Kim Blair, Director of MIT Center for Sports Innovation, USA**

↑ The shape and flexibility of materials used in the bike, and the clothes and position of the rider, can be adjusted by sports engineers to improve a cyclist's performance.

What skills do I need?

Many sports engineers have a degree in mechanical engineering, sports technology, materials science or medical physics. Others take the longer route of starting with an engineering apprenticeship or diploma and then becoming a technician assisting an engineer. All these qualifications demand science, maths and practical skills. It may be helpful to get some experience by working as an intern at a sports engineering centre or company.

Sports agent

Sport is big business and sports stars need experts to help them negotiate issues such as salaries and the right team to play for. These experts are sports agents.

Sports agents often work for several talented clients. They help each one to get signed with a sports team, club or organisation for the highest possible salary and also with the best prospects for advancing their long-term career. Agents liaise with players, managers, team owners and lawyers. In addition, they negotiate sponsorship deals with equipment manufacturers and act as media spokespeople for their clients.

← Agents often earn a percentage of their client's commission, so they also benefit if they can get their athlete a good salary or sponsorship deal.

What skills do I need?

A good sports agent will spend a lot of time with their clients, discussing career goals and timescales and weighing up options. A sports star is a brand. To be successful, you will need to be able to market them to potential clubs. This requires excellent communication and persuasive skills. Some sports agents have a degree in law or business studies, but they can also take diplomas to develop the legal and maths skills required to understand contracts.

→

Sports agents need patience.
It can take a long time to get
the right deals for their clients.

Job description

Sports agents:
- promote sportspeople to clubs or organisations that may be interested in signing them
- handle contracts and salary negotiations
- deal with additional commercial opportunities, such as sponsorship and product endorsements
- advise clients on strategies to develop their careers
- attend sports matches and events that their clients are taking part in.

Sports coach

The job of a sports coach is to get athletes, players and teams ready for competition. They instruct, train and motivate people to reach their full potential and take part safely in their chosen sport.

Job description

Sports coaches:
• plan and run sports training sessions, from gym work to shooting practice, to develop fitness, skills and knowledge
• evaluate sporting performances for athletes and advise on any changes required
• monitor the physical condition, lifestyle and mental attitude of those taking part in the sport
• develop players to help build effective squads
• go to competitions and events with participants, and sometimes select team members.

← Sports coaches decide on team formation and tactics, planning how to win matches and competitions.

Different types of sports coach

Coaches are also known as instructors or trainers. They may support professional sportspeople as well as community teams or school groups. Sports coaches usually specialise in one sport or activity – for example, basketball or gymnastics. Some teams have several specialist coaches, such as a pitching and a batting coach for a baseball team. Only a few sports coaches do the job full-time – most are part-time employees or volunteers.

Coaches are vital during an event to spur performers on, so that they perform at their best.

PROFESSIONAL VIEWPOINT
'Coaches should be open to new ideas, willing to share knowledge and help others, have a passion for and good knowledge of their sport, be a friend and a role model to the players, and be happy to work unsociable hours.'
Stephen King, sports coach

What skills do I need?

To become a sports coach, you will need to be physically fit, well organised and a natural leader who can encourage others to perform and improve. You should gain a coaching qualification that is recognised by the national governing body for your sport. If you are interested in coaching as a career, why not volunteer to help coach a school or local team for a few hours a week, to gain useful experience?

Athlete

Do you think you have the exceptional talent, drive and determination required to become an athlete? Most athletes are amateurs. They may compete at the highest level but still rely on a second career to earn money. Very few are good enough, or lucky enough, to become professionals.

Athletes need dedication to train hard so they can get stronger and fitter and perform at the highest level.

Job description

Athletes:

- compete in matches and competitions
- improve their skills with regular practice
- maintain their fitness with training and gym sessions
- manage their diet and lifestyle
- review their own and opposition performances with coaches and team managers
- attend press conferences and give interviews before and after matches.

↑ However fit you are, sporting technique and skills can make the difference between winning and losing.

Athletes compete in individual sports such as athletics or horse racing, or in team sports like cricket or ice hockey. They work alongside other people such as coaches, psychologists, nutritionists and agents who advise them on many aspects of their lives, from what they eat to how they should train. Some sportspeople earn regular salaries, but others only get paid if they do well in competitions.

PROFESSIONAL VIEWPOINT

'Work as hard as you possibly can, while ensuring any practice you do is beneficial and specific. Take the time to think about the game and different situations, and always be willing to learn from other people and experiences you may have. Most of all, believe in your ability and your mental approach to make the most of your skills.'

Will Smith, professional cricketer

What skills do I need?

Many sports professionals are 'spotted' early on by a talent scout for a professional sports team when playing at an amateur club. You will probably have plenty of skills and awareness of tactics and be competitive and fit. But it is important to keep building your skills, strength and stamina by constantly training and learning in order to succeed at the top level of a sport.

Glossary

abseiling controlled slide down a fixed rope used by mountaineers

acupuncture inserting thin needles into the skin to treat pain or illness

aerobics rhythmic, intense exercise to work the muscles and heart, increasing fitness

amputee someone who has lost one or more limbs through illness or accident

carbon fibre stiff, light and strong material

computer modelling using computer programs to create three-dimensional images of objects – for example, to predict how they respond to strong forces

commentate to report on an event as it occurs, especially for a news or sports broadcast

diagnose to investigate the cause or nature of a condition, situation or problem

fouling breaking the rules of a sport, sometimes causing injury to another player

freelancer someone who works independently, for different employers

intern someone who spends time working for an employer to learn skills needed for a job

liaise to talk to or communicate with people so they can work together

life-saving technique way of keeping a serious casualty alive by making sure they are breathing and their heart is beating

manipulation when physiotherapists use their hands to move limbs – for example, to increase joint mobility

marketing the business of finding out what people want to buy and how to sell things to them

negotiate to arrange a mutually agreed outcome, such as a salary

nutritionist professional who advises on diet planning for weight loss, medical or health reasons

officiate to serve as an official or authority

physiotherapy exercising specific parts of the body to regain movement or ease pain

product endorsement public statement, usually by a well-known person, recommending a particular product

prototype first sample or model

public relations (PR) the business of promoting a favourable relationship with the public – for example, through advertising and publicity

referred when care of a patient is transferred to another medical specialist

rehabilitation restoring someone to a healthy condition – for example, using physiotherapy to regain movement after injury

simulate to imitate or copy

spinning exercise programme using a stationary bike in a gym

sports fixture sports match or event

stamina energy and strength to endure lengthy physical activity

statistics data, interpreted using maths in order to make predictions or spot trends

strain to injure a muscle or other body part through over-exertion or an accident

treadmill exercise machine with a moving belt, used to run or walk on the spot

ultrasound using sound waves to warm and treat injured body parts such as joints

velodrome stadium with angled track for cycle racing

visualisation of success training to create mental images of success that help someone achieve actual success

Zumba dance fitness exercise programme

Further information

There are many specific courses, apprenticeships and jobs using sports skills, so where do you go to find out more? It is really useful to meet up with careers advisers at school or college and to attend careers fairs to see the range of opportunities. Remember that public libraries and newspapers are other important sources of information. The earlier you check out your options, the better prepared you will be to put your sporting skills to good use as you earn a living in future.

Books

Being a Pro Footballer (Radar Top Jobs), Sarah Levete, Wayland, 2013

Career Ideas for Kids Who Like Sports (Career Ideas for Kids), Diane Lindsey Reeves, Lindsey Clasen and Nancy Bond, Checkmark Books, 2007

Coaches and Fitness Professionals (Ferguson's Careers in Focus), Facts on File, 2008

What's It Like to Be a Sports Trainer? (On the Job), Elizabeth Pickard and Lisa Thompson, A&C Black, 2008

Yes, She Can!: Women's Sports Pioneers (Good Sports), Glenn Stout, Houghton Mifflin, 2011

Websites

www.careers-in-sport.co.uk
The Careers in Sport website includes in-depth descriptions of different jobs using sports skills, interviews with people in the sports industry and lots more useful information.

www.sportscoachuk.org/coaches/ i-want-coach
Are you interested in being a sports coach? Then you should visit this website to find out more.

https://nationalcareersservice.direct. gov.uk/advice/planning/jobfamily/Pages/ sportleisureandtourism.aspx
There is a much wider range of jobs using sports skills than can be covered in this book. To get an idea of the range, visit this website.

www.exploratorium.edu/explore/staff_ picks/sports_science
Learn a little more about sports science by trying some of the activities on this website.

Index

I'M GOOD AT...

Contents of all the titles in the series:

WAYLAND